For Janet ~ M. H.

For my family and friends ~ C. C.

VIKING
Published by the Penguin Group
Penguin Putnam Inc., 375 Hudson Street, New York, New York 10014, U.S.A.
Penguin Books Ltd, 27 Wrights Lane, London W8 5TZ, England
Penguin Books Australia Ltd, Ringwood, Victoria, Australia
Penguin Books Canada Ltd, 10 Alcorn Avenue, Toronto, Ontario, Canada M4V 3B2
Penguin Books (N.Z.) Ltd, 182-190 Wairau Road, Auckland 10, New Zealand

Penguin Books Ltd, Registered Offices: Harmondsworth, Middlesex, England

First published in Great Britain by Frances Lincoln Ltd., 1998
First published in the United States by Viking,
a member of Penguin Putnam Inc., 1998

1 3 5 7 9 10 8 6 4 2

Text copyright © Meredith Hooper, 1998
Illustrations copyright © Christopher Coady, 1998
All rights reserved

Library of Congress Catalog Card Number: 97-61733
ISBN 0-670-87618-6

The author and publishers would like to thank the following for their professional advice:
Professor Richard Wayne, Physical and Theoretical Chemistry Laboratory,
Oxford University; Dr. Geoff Jenkins, Royal Meteorological Society;
Dr. Wendy Kirk, Department of Geological Science, University College, London.

Printed in Hong Kong
Set in Goudy

The Drop in My Drink

The Story of Water on Our Planet

MEREDITH HOOPER

illustrated by CHRIS COADY

VIKING

A drop of water is made up of billions and billions
of unimaginably small water molecules.
Every drop of water is a different collection
of these molecules, because water is
constantly moving, re-forming, recycling.

The Drop in My Drink *tells the story of water—*
where it came from, how it behaves, why it matters.
Each new drop in my drink is a different drop,
but each drop can stand for any drop and every drop.

At the back of this book there is a diagram of the
water cycle, and some amazing facts about water.

Water trickles and seeps and flows. It freezes into hard ice.
It floats in the air. It is liquid and solid and vapor.
It is never still.

Little drops of water drip from the tap. Where did you
come from, drop of water?

Water dribbles down rocks. Water churns along rivers and fills great oceans. Water tumbles inside clouds, drifts as snowflakes, collects in puddles. Water creeps up the stems of sunflowers and slips down the throats of tigers. It's all the same water. The water our Earth began with.

A lot of water is stored in the universe. Ice, dust, and rock make up many of the bodies whizzing and tumbling through space. Earth formed when small lumps and large lumps of matter pounded into each other, clumping and fusing together. The lumps contained water trapped between grains of rock, and water frozen into ice.

As the new planet heated up, then cooled, water was released.
Clouds of vapor and gases rose from Earth's thin crust.
Comets crashing into Earth's surface brought more water.

Earth is 4.6 billion years old. But the drop in my drink
is even older.

All the water we have is all the water we've always had.

Earth is a very watery planet. Almost all of Earth's water is salty, filling the seas and oceans which wash and swirl over its surface.

Only a little bit of Earth's water is fresh, and up to three quarters of that is frozen as ice. Fresh water falls from the sky as rain, snow, or hail, much of it straight into the sea. The fresh water that falls onto land mostly soaks into the ground and disappears.

Earth's surface sucks up water like a huge sponge. The water travels slowly down through soil and rock, sometimes leaking out into springs, streams, or squelchy bogs. A very small part of the fresh water runs across the ground into rivers and lakes.

The drop in my drink has been in all the world's oceans. It has been in mighty rivers and icy glaciers. It has been in clear mountain lakes and six miles down inside the Earth.

Hundreds of millions of millions of tons of water float in the sky. Water rises as an invisible gas, water vapor, drawn into the air by the sun's heat. It rises from muddy earth, rockpools, and rivers, from leaves and melting snow and the surface of the ocean.

Water vapor is always present in the air. As air rises, water vapor cools and condenses around microscopic particles to form minute droplets of water, making clouds, white fluffy clouds or dark towering clouds. High in the atmosphere, water vapor condenses into tiny crystals of ice, making thin wispy clouds.

Winds carry water vapor, water droplets, and ice crystals through the atmosphere. Somewhere, sometime, some will fall back down from clouds as rain, hail, or snow.

Water goes up and back and up and back,
endlessly evaporating and purifying, endlessly
condensing and recycling. But the water in
the atmosphere is never more than one
thousandth of one percent of all the water
on Earth.

Carried by winds, the drop in my drink has whizzed across continents.
It has howled six miles above mountains in icy jetstreams. It has been
dragged violently up and down through thunderclouds, growing layers
of ice, and hurtled to the ground as hailstones. The drop in my drink
has been an endless number of raindrops.

Life on Earth began in water, and all life stayed in the water for 3 billion years. For much of that time every living thing was tiny, single-celled, and simple.

The drop in my drink helped life on Earth begin.

Little multicelled animals lived on muddy seabeds 530 million years ago. Some had five eyes, nozzles like vacuum cleaners, and backward-facing mouths.

The drop in my drink has carried the bodies of creatures whose shapes and designs have disappeared forever.

Some plants managed to move out of the water about 450 million years ago, but they could only survive in wet ground. Then plants developed roots which reached down through the soil, searching for moisture.

Plants cannot live without water. Water fills them, like containers. Water gives them shape, and helps make and carry their food.

The drop in my drink has been inside the first plants that lived in the sea, and the first plants that lived on dry land.

Some animals moved out of the water to creep over the land around 390 million years ago. The first were wormlike, and wore their skeletons on the outside. Later, animals with backbones, four legs, and wet skins began clambering over the land. All the animals had to develop new ways of breathing and moving on land. But wherever they were, they had to find supplies of water to stay alive.

Salty swamps and stinking bogs bordered the edges of a shallow inland sea 75 million years ago. The sun shone hot. Not much rain fell. But slow-moving, weed-covered streams fed into the swamps, and here hadrosaurs lived, drinking the fresh water.

Water is the major part of every living thing on Earth. The drop in my drink has been inside millions of living things.

The drop in my drink has fed the tallest trees and the smallest flowers.

Rain poured onto a rain forest 15 million years ago. Water drops dripped past a python coiled around a branch, trickled down tangled vines through ferns and fungi to the forest floor, and seeped into the soil. The water drops were absorbed by the tiny hairs on a tree root and carried back up, up through the mighty trunk of the forest tree to the leaves—and sent back out into the air as vapor, from where they fell again as rain onto the rain forest and dribbled back down a tree trunk onto the forest floor.

Water helps make the food that plants and animals need. It helps move the food around their systems and get rid of their waste products. All plants and animals must take in water to replace the water they give out. Without water, there would be no life on our planet.

Rain drums on hillsides, prying off loose fragments of rock. Rivers cut away the soil of their banks. Waves smash against cliffs, wearing down coastlines. Ice pries open cracks. Endlessly, tirelessly, water attacks Earth's surface, slamming into it, breaking things off, dissolving, weathering, changing.

Water and ice drag gravel, sand, and silt endlessly downward. Shifting, stripping, scraping, grinding. Eroding, rearranging.

The drop in my drink is a miniature crowbar. It has moved mountains. It has made valleys. It has carved coasts.

But every time the drop revisits the land, the land is different. Because other drops have changed it.

Caves under the earth lead one into another,
great, dark, silent spaces inside the rock. Cold
rivers run along hidden channels.

Light shines through a hole in a cave roof.
White heaps of bones lie on the cave floor.
Two million years ago animals ran across the
land above. Some stumbled through the hole
and fell in. Bones falling on bones.

The drop in my drink has carved out caves.
It has dripped through a cave's limestone ceiling,
leaving a tiny new speck on the point of a stalactite.
The drop in my drink has dissolved rock, making
new substances.

The drop in my drink journeys constantly between land, sea, and sky. It can stay for ten days in the atmosphere. Two weeks in a river. Ten years in a lake. It can stay a few weeks or 10,000 years underground, ancient rain waiting to move again. But always it moves on.

One hundred and twenty thousand years ago, the drop in my drink fell as powder snow in the icy silence of the South Pole. It blew along the surface of the great ice sheet, then changed under the weight of snow heaped above it into solid, blue glacier ice. It slipped and scraped over buried mountains, as the ice sheet shifted and ground towards the ocean. The drop in my drink traveled inside the ice sheet for more than 100,000 years.

At the edge of the land, great pieces of ice sheet break off into the sea as icebergs.

The drop in my drink has been inside an iceberg floating its white bulk in the cold blue ocean, slowly melting.

Waves roar into the iceberg's ice caves. The edges of the iceberg crumble, it wallows and tilts, and all the ancient snowflakes fizz and melt into the sea.

Four thousand years ago the drop in my drink sank down through the cold Southern Ocean.

Giant pale squid swam through it, searching for prey. Deep-diving whales gulped it, searching for squid.

Four miles down, in the darkness of the deepest water, it joined a current of very cold, very salty water flowing through the world's oceans.

The drop in my drink rose into the clear, warm, sunlit shallows of a coral reef.

It carried food to the stinging tentacles of small coral polyps. It was sucked through the bright bodies of sea squirts, and around the arms of starfish. It lapped the eyes of a turtle and the fin of a shark.

Two years ago the drop in my drink evaporated from the top of a wave, traveled a quarter of the way around the world in a week, clashed in a storm, fell in a shower of rain on wet hills, and trickled down glistening rocks into a stream which fed into a river.

The drop spun and tumbled in the river's current, carrying particles of clay, grains of sand and microscopic animals, until it fed into the quiet water of a reservoir.

It touched the shiny scales of fish, the stems of green plants. Leaves and dust sank down through it. It was swallowed by small organisms and pushed out again. It did not evaporate back up into the sky.

A few weeks ago my drop was pumped through strainers
and filters to remove large things and microscopic things.
It was blown through the air, mixed with chemicals to kill
microorganisms, and fed into pipes buried under the ground.
A second ago the drop was in my tap.

Water drips from the tap in slow, clear drops. I catch a drop in my glass.

My drop has been salty seawater and fresh, clear rainwater. It has been hail and dew, ice and water vapor. It has tossed in deep oceans and flowed in great rivers. It has worn down the surface of the planet and reshaped it.

My drop has fed tall trees and creeping grasses, the tiniest insect and the largest animal. It has been inside eagles and crocodiles, worms and spiders, fish and elephants. It has been inside long strands of seaweed and prickly desert cactus and an apple tree. It has been inside an Egyptian princess and a Tyrannosaurus rex.

My drop of water is older than our planet. Each tiny part of water inside my drop has its own amazing history. But all the tiny parts have joined together for the first time in this drop.

My drop of water is as young as this moment.

This drop happened just for me.

Looking After Water

Every living thing on our planet depends on water. Every organism is endlessly thirsty. Water is the most important substance we have. It carries dissolved food to plants and animals, and removes waste products. It helps shape Earth's surface, control its temperature, and create the weather. Almost everything on Earth happens the way it does because of liquid water.

We humans depend utterly on water to survive. But we have always used water for other purposes: to clean the things we eat and use, and to carry away our dirt and trash. Increasingly, we are using water for industry and agriculture. Now toxic wastes, pesticides, and fertilizers are contaminating and polluting water supplies.

Water cleans itself naturally as it travels. But water is never completely "pure." Water is extremely good at carrying things and dissolving things, so it is always adding to itself. Almost everything finds its way into water in the end, but not everything that needs to be taken out is being removed.

People everywhere in the world need fresh, clean water. As water above the ground becomes polluted, supplies of fresh water under the ground are being removed. People mine for water, taking out quickly what can only be renewed very slowly.

We risk altering the natural balances which preserve the planet's water supplies. We are putting pressure on the future.

Our planet's precious water should not be wasted. It must be protected. It's all the water we have.

The Water Cycle

The water cycle is a huge natural process. Water on our planet is always moving and changing, and always renewing itself. Water freezes into ice sheets and collects in snowbanks. It fills lakes, rivers, and seas. It seeps into the ground, traveling slowly through soil and rock. Some of this water evaporates, rising into the atmosphere as water vapor, where it cools and condenses. It falls again as rain, snow, and hail or settles as frost, fog, and dew onto the land and the sea.

At the same time, all living things take in water and pass it out again, as liquid and as vapor.

All the water that leaves the surface of our earth comes back to earth in one form or another.

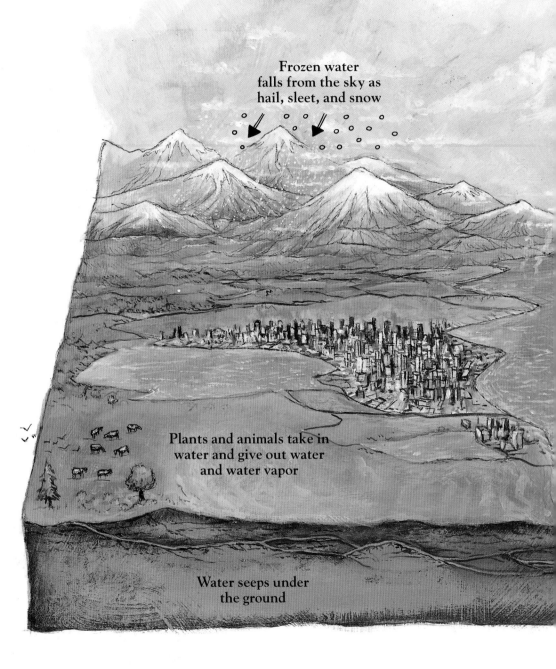

Frozen water falls from the sky as hail, sleet, and snow

Plants and animals take in water and give out water and water vapor

Water seeps under the ground

Water vapor
rises and cools,
forming clouds

Water droplets
fall from the
clouds as rain

Water evaporates
from rivers, lakes,
and oceans

Amazing Water Facts

 If all the water in the atmosphere fell
at once, it would cover the surface of the
planet in one inch of rain.

 At any one time clouds cover about half
the Earth, but only 5% turn into rain, hail,
and snow.

 An average puffy white cloud weighs
about 400 tons and contains about as much
water as an Olympic swimming pool.

 Oceans and seas cover approximately
70% of the Earth's surface.

 The icecap covering Antarctica averages
1.3 miles thick, and contains about 60–70%
of all Earth's fresh water.

 Human beings are leaky bags of water.
Two-thirds (about 66%) of an average
adult's body weight is water.

 A chicken is 74% water, a herring
67%, an earthworm 80%.

 Plants are largely water—a tomato
is 95% water, an apple 80%.

 On a warm day, a birch tree takes
up to 20 gallons of water from the soil,
pushing it out into the air as vapor
through its 250,000 leaves.

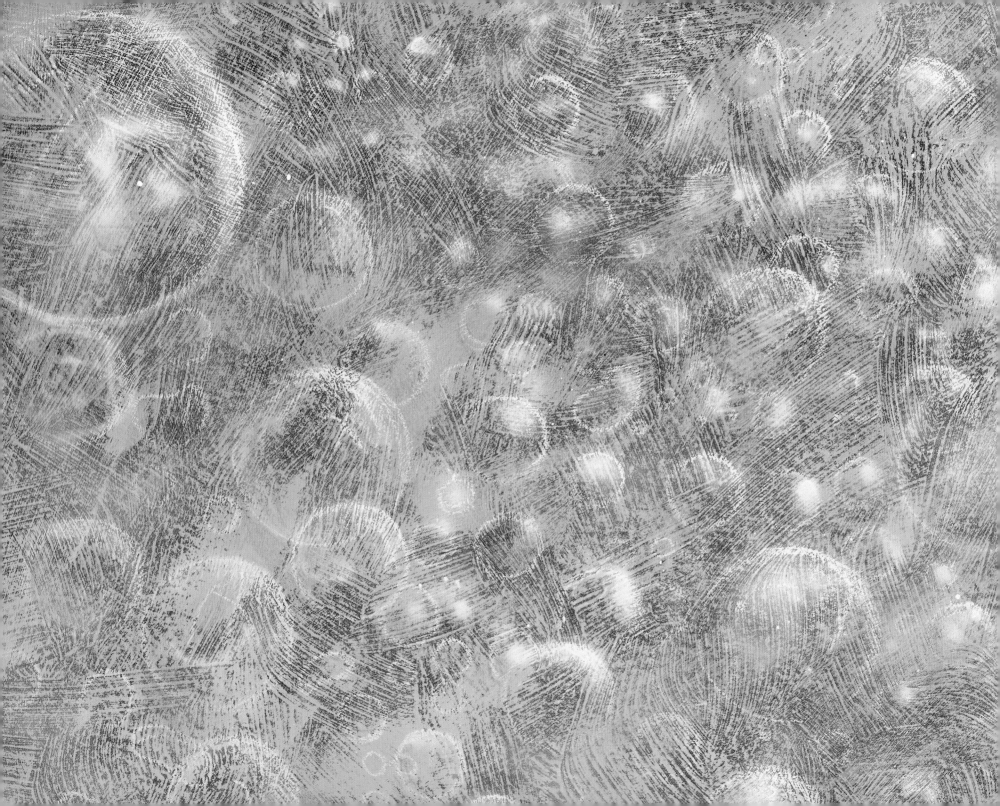